Enchanting Fairy Tales

Retold by Jim Lawrence

MODERN PUBLISHING
A Division of Unisystems, Inc.
New York, New York 10022
Printed in Mexico

CONTENTS

The Three Pigs

Once there was a mama pig and her three little baby pigs. When her sons were old enough to leave home, the mama pig told them to watch out for the bad wolf.

"He's full of tricks, and he would just *love* a fat little pig for dinner!" she warned.

"Don't worry, Mama," they said. "We'll be careful!"

Soon after he started out, the first little pig met a man carrying a load of straw.

"Just the stuff to make a pretty little house with!" said the foolish piggy. So he bought some and built himself a house of straw.

A little while later, he heard a knock on the door. "Who's there?" he called.

"Your friendly next-door neighbor," said a low, sweet voice.

But the little pig peeked out and saw that it was really the wolf!

"May I come in?" the bad wolf smirked.

"No, not by the hair of my chinny-chin-chin!"

"Then I'll huff and I'll puff and I'll *blo-o-ow* your house down!" roared the wolf. And so he did!

Meanwhile, the second little pig met a man with a load of wooden sticks. "What a fine house I can build with those!" he exclaimed. So he bought some and built himself a wooden house.

Just then his brother came running and told about his narrow escape from the wolf.

Soon they heard a knock on the door.

"Hello, neighbor!" the wolf purred sweetly. "May I come in?"

"No, not by the hair of my chinny-chin-chin!" cried the second little pig.

"Then I'll huff and I'll puff and I'll *blo-o-ow* your house down!" roared the wolf.

Those two little pigs barely had time to jump out the window and run before the house came tumbling down around their ears!

But the third little pig was much smarter
than his two brothers. He built *his* house
out of bricks. Oh, how glad they were to
run there and hide!

Soon they heard a knock on the door.
"May I come in?" asked the wolf.

"No, not by the hair of my chinny-chin-chin!" said the third little pig.

"Then I'll huff and I'll puff and I'll *blo-o-ow* your house down!" roared the wolf.

"Go right ahead," the piggy dared him.

The wolf huffed and puffed and blew till he was red in the face, but the brick house just stood there. It didn't even shake.

The wolf howled with rage. "Don't think you three ninnies will get away this time!" he snarled. "I'll come down the chimney and gobble you all up!"

"Fine, come right ahead!" the third little pig invited him. And while he was talking, the pig built a blazing fire in the fireplace and put a big pot of water on to boil.

The wolf climbed up on the roof, licking his chops. He could hardly wait to sink his teeth into those fat little piggies. What a fine dinner they would make! His mouth was watering as he squirmed down the chimney.

Down he slid . . . into you-know-what! "*Yeoww! Wowww!*" screeched the wolf as he landed, *KER-SPLASH*, in the boiling water!

The wolf immediately jumped out and
ran out the window. He never returned and
bothered the three pigs again.

Goldilocks and the Three Bears

Once upon a time there was a little girl named Goldilocks who went for a walk in the woods one morning. Her mama had often told her never to do that by herself—but Goldilocks didn't mind her very well.

Much to her surprise, she came to a pretty little house deep among the trees. "Hmm, I wonder who lives there?" she said softly.

No sooner had the question crossed her mind than she decided to find out. Goldilocks never worried over whether she should or shouldn't do a certain thing—she just did as she pleased.

She walked up to the house and knocked. No one answered. Goldilocks tried the latch and found out the door was open, so without a moment's hesitation, she went right inside.

On one side of the house was the kitchen, and on the other side was the parlor.

In the kitchen, on a table, were three different-sized bowls of porridge.

"Mmm, that smells good!" murmured Goldilocks, who was feeling quite hungry from her long walk in the open air. "I think I'll try some!"

So she dipped a spoon into the biggest bowl. "*Oooh!*" she cried. The porridge was much too hot and almost burned her lips.

Then she tried the middle-sized bowl. The porridge in that one was too cold to please Goldilocks.

But the porridge in the littlest bowl tasted just right—not too cold and not too hot. So Goldilocks ate it all up.

Now, her tummy nice and full, Goldilocks went into the parlor and found three different-sized chairs. They all looked so comfy that Goldilocks decided to sit down and rest a bit before she left.

First she tried the biggest chair. When she sat in it, her legs weren't long enough to reach the floor. In fact, she couldn't even bend her knees—her feet just stuck out over the edge.

"Hmph, this one's no good!" Goldilocks decided.

The middle-sized chair wasn't much better—her feet still couldn't reach the floor.

But the littlest chair was just the right size. Goldilocks was so pleased she rocked back and forth in it and bounced up and down on the cushion. But she rocked and bounced so hard that the chair broke, and Goldilocks landed, *plop*, on the floor!

She didn't like that a bit and almost started to cry. But then she decided that if she could just lie down for a while, she might feel well enough to go home.

Upstairs she found a bedroom with three different-sized beds. The biggest bed was too hard to lie on comfortably. The middle-sized one was too soft. But the littlest one felt just right. It was so comfy, Goldilocks fell fast asleep.

Guess who lived in that house? *Three Bears!* A big Daddy Bear and a middle-sized Mama Bear and a little wee Baby Bear. They had just gone out to gather some honey for breakfast while their porridge cooled.

Goldilocks hadn't even shut the door tight, so they knew right away that someone had been there while they were gone.

In the kitchen they got another unpleasant surprise.

"Someone's been eating my porridge!" growled the Daddy Bear in a big deep voice.

"Someone's been eating *my* porridge!" the Mama Bear chimed in.

"Someone's been eating my porridge, and they gobbled it all up!" cried the little wee Baby Bear.

In the parlor, the big Daddy Bear saw that the slipcover on his favorite chair was wrinkled.

"Someone's been sitting in my chair!" he rumbled angrily.

"And someone's been sitting in *my* chair!" echoed the Mama Bear.

"Someone's been sitting in my chair," wailed the Baby Bear, "*and broke it all apart!*"

By now, the big Daddy Bear was scowling furiously. He marched upstairs—*thump, thump, thump*—to see what else they might find and . . . *oh, oh!*

"Someone's been sleeping in my bed!" he thundered.

23

"Someone's been sleeping in *my* bed!" Mama Bear complained.

But the Baby Bear let out a startled yelp. "Someone's been sleeping in my bed—AND HERE SHE IS!"

The noise woke up Goldilocks. When she saw the Three Bears looking at her, she almost fainted with fright!

Jumping out of bed, she scampered downstairs and out the door, and ran all the way home without even looking back once, for fear the Three Bears were right behind her!

(Goldilocks minds Mama much better now.)

The Ugly Duckling

Springtime had come and as the days grew warmer, the storks came flying back from Africa and circled over their summer home in the north, a lovely old stone castle.

Its walls were lapped by a gentle stream whose waters flowed into a calm blue lake that was surrounded by tall reeds and green foliage.

Ducks and other water fowl swam on the lake, enjoying the glorious spring sunshine. But on one bank, a mother duck sat on her nest, waiting patiently for her eggs to hatch.

At last came the great day! One by one, her fluffy little ducklings broke out of their shells and toddled about, saying, *"Cheep, cheep!"* with their little yellow bills. Such fun they had, exploring the world for the first time!

"Ah, how good it'll feel to stretch my legs," sighed Mama Duck. "Now I can take a refreshing dip in the water—and you, my little ones, all need a good bath!"

Then she noticed that the biggest egg of all hadn't hatched yet. "Oh dear," she thought, tapping it with her beak. "I hope it's not a turkey egg. I got fooled that way once before—and the little thing couldn't even swim!"

Nevertheless, being a good mother bird, she stayed in her nest, watching her little darlings, until the big egg also hatched. But what a strange-looking creature broke out of the shell! It had dull gray feathers and a huge beak.

Mama Duck scarcely knew what to make of her new baby. "Maybe it's a turkey, after all," she thought. "It's surely too ugly to be a duck! . . . Oh well, we shall soon find out. This one's going to learn to swim if I have to *push* him in the water!"

The next morning, Mama Duck took h brood down to the shore. Her downy yellow ducklings took to the water happily and paddled about with their little webbe feet as if they'd been swimming all their lives.

The big one didn't have to be pushed either. It jumped right in and held its ne up straight and swam around the best an fastest of all.

Mama Duck felt better as she watched it. "He may be ugly," she thought, "but he looks strong and brave, and I shall lo him as much as any of the others."

Now that her children were all clean,
she led them into the farmyard to
introduce them to society.

The yard echoed with noisy clucking and
squawking. Two hens were fighting over a
fishhead when the farm cat suddenly ran
up and snatched it away from both of
them.

Mama Duck paid no attention to such
ill-bred behavior. The important thing was
that her own young ones learned proper
manners. She told them to bow to their
elders and walk with their toes pointed
outward, as good little ducks should.

All the noise quieted down as she led her little troop into the yard. The other ducks and chickens and geese crowded around to admire her new family.

"Oh, what pretty babies!" cooed a lady duck.

"But what's that homely gray thing doing at the beginning of the line?" said another. And the whole barnyard burst out laughing.

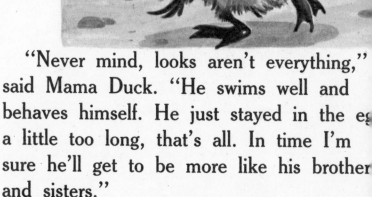

"Never mind, looks aren't everything," said Mama Duck. "He swims well and behaves himself. He just stayed in the egg a little too long, that's all. In time I'm sure he'll get to be more like his brother and sisters."

"Excuses won't help matters," blustered a big, red-faced turkey gobbler. "We don't want any ugly, misshapen creatures like him ruining our neighborhood!"

And with that, the turkey gobbler puffed out its wings and feathers and came flying angrily at the poor gray duckling and even pecked it on the head.

The others treated him just as badly, saying they wouldn't let their children play with such a freak of nature.

Mama Duck tried to defend her odd-looking child, but it was no use. Every fowl in the farmyard seemed to have it in for the ugly duckling. They pecked and bullied him from morning till night.

His brothers and sisters were embarrassed to have such a relative. "The cat should get you, funny face!" they chirped whenever he tried to join in their games.

Even the milkmaid kicked him out of her way when she came into the barnyard to feed the poultry.

The poor duckling was so unhappy that at last he couldn't stand it any longer. "No one wants me around here," he gloomed. "I may as well run away!"

But first he had to flutter and poke h[is] way through the bushes around the farmyard. In doing so, he startled some little birds who flew up, chirping and twittering with fright.

"Even they can't stand the sight of me!" thought the ugly duckling. And his heart felt so sad and heavy that he tuck[ed] his little head under his wing and cried.

In the gathering dusk, he toddled dow[n] to the lake and hid in the reedy marsh.

When he woke up the next morning, there were two wild ducks staring at him. "What's this funny-looking thing?" asked one.

The duckling bowed and tried to expla[in] who he was, but they just stared all the [more] harder. "A duck?" quacked the other. "[You] must be joking!"

Just then some wild geese flew overhead. They honked down at the overgrown youngster, inviting him to join them.

"They're just making fun of me,"
thought the duckling, feeling lonelier than
ever. "Why would they want a freak like
me in their fl—"

BOOM! . . . BANG!

Two of the flock came tumbling down
out of the sky. Hunters had just shot
them!

Then a gun dog went splashing by through the marsh to pick up the fallen goosey-ganders. The hairy beast saw the frightened little fowl hiding and trembling in the reeds, but didn't even stop to give it a sniff.

"He probably thinks such an ugly morsel as me would make him sick," the duckling said to himself.

All summer long, the poor homeless youngster wandered about the shore, pecking up whatever bits of food he could find in the marsh.

Autumn drew near, and the leaves turned yellow.

One cold, windy evening he came to a broken-down cabin where an old woman lived with her hen and tomcat.

Her eyes were dim and she took him in, thinking he was a lady duck who might lay her some tasty duck eggs.

But the duckling, of course, could do nothing of the kind.

"What good are you, anyhow, if you can't catch mice like me," sneered the tomcat, "or lay eggs like my friend, Mrs. Hen?"

"I c-c-can swim," stammered the duckling timidly. "You've no idea how nice it is, paddling about the lake or diving down through the cool water to the soft green weeds on the bottom!"

"Hmph! Paddling and diving, indeed!" the hen scolded. "Do you suppose the old woman or friend Tom here or I are stupid enough to go swimming in all that water? If you don't know any better than that, you may as well leave right now!"

"Yeah, butt out, you homely young no-good!" hissed the cat. "We were better off before you came!"

So once again the ugly duckling had to fend for himself. The days grew shorter and darker, and the leaves fell from the trees. Squirrels hurried to line their nests for the winter.

One evening, when the duckling went swimming as the sun was going down, he heard a loud beating of wings. Great lovely white birds, the largest he had ever seen, were flying overhead.

The duckling felt a strange pang as he listened to their happy cries. If only he, too, could be so strong and free!

He stretched out his little neck and tried to answer them, but the only sound that came out was a hoarse, scary little squawk. Frightened and ashamed, the duckling dived deep down out of sight.

When he came up, he knew that nothing could ever take away the memory of those beautiful creatures. "Never mind if I'm so ugly that no one can bear to be around me," he thought. "I shall love them always, with all my heart!"

Winter came on, and soon the first snowflakes fluttered from the sky. The duckling shivered in the cold. He had to keep swimming around to prevent his spot on the lake from freezing. It was no use. One night in the bitter cold he found it harder and harder to paddle with his little webbed feet. By morning he was frozen fast in the ice!

Thank goodness a peasant saw his plight. With one of his wooden shoes, he broke the poor creature free from the ice and took it home to his cottage, under his coat.

His children made a great fuss over their new pet. They rubbed it back to life with warm cloths and wanted to play with it. But the poor duckling was frightened out of his wits by all the noise and excitement.

36

He fluttered about so wildly that he knocked over a milk pail and fell into the flour bin. The children laughed and clapped their hands, and the peasant's angry wife came at him with a broom. The duckling barely managed to escape out the door and fell exhausted in the snow.

Oh, what a terrible time he had that winter! There was so little to eat that he nearly starved, and he huddled out of the wind as best he could through the long, freezing nights.

At last the sunshine grew warmer. Spring had arrived once again. In some strange way, the duckling had changed and no longer felt like his former self. His neck had grown long and slim, and his wings seemed immense.

He tried flapping them a bit. How strong they were! To his amazement, he felt himself rising off the ground, higher and higher into the air.

"I'm flying!" he thought. "Now I really *am* strong and free!"

In his happiness, he could have flown on forever, but he swooped down at last toward a flowering garden on the shore of a lovely blue lake.

Suddenly his heart skipped a beat. Three beautiful birds came swimming out of the reeds and bushes—the same glorious creatures he had glimpsed flying south in the sunset, months ago!

A daring thought flashed through his mind. "Now's my chance," he decided, "to greet them face to face—just this once! After that, it won't matter if they make fun of my ugliness and drive me away—at least I shall always remember this moment!"

The lovely white swans came gliding toward him, swift as arrows. He bent his head humbly, expecting them to peck him and beat him with their wings.

Then he saw something so startling, he couldn't understand it. What was that great white creature doing, swimming upside down in the water? Was it another of the flock, coming up from the bottom of the lake to drive him away?

No, it was his own reflection! He, too, was a handsome, snow-white swan!

And now the other swans, instead of driving him away, were greeting him fondly

A boy and a girl had come down to the shore to throw crumbs to the birds. "Look at the new swan!" cried the girl. "He's the most beautiful of all!"

Even the little squirrels in the bushes chattered with admiration.

The wonder of it all made him dizzy with joy. His heart beat so fast, it felt ready to burst. In his confusion, he tucked his head under his wing and remembered all the sad, painful things that had happened to him since he first broke out of his shell.

But all that lay in the past. Now he was one of those strong, graceful creatures—the most beautiful bird of the air—a *swan!*

Raising his head again, he gazed up into the blue sky and his heart swelled. "I never dreamed I could ever find so much happiness," he said to himself, "when I was just an Ugly Duckling!"

Puss in Boots

Once upon a time, a miller had three sons. When the miller died, he left his mill to his oldest son, his donkey to his second son, and his cat to his youngest son.

The youngest son felt very down -in-the- mouth. "My oldest brother has a mill for grinding corn," he grumbled, "and my second brother has a donkey that can carry heavy loads to market, but how am I going to make my living when all I have in the world is a cat?"

"Cheer up, Master," said the cat. "Just get me a hat and a pair of leather boots, and I promise you, your fortune will soon be made!"

Well, the youth felt better when he heard that, because he knew this was a very smart cat. So he did as Puss asked and got him a plumed hat and a jaunty pair of boots.

Then the cat put a couple of carrots and some lettuce in a bag and went out into the fields and lay down beside it, with the bag wide open, pretending to be dead.

Soon a plump rabbit came creeping up. He sniffed the tempting veggies and started to gobble them as fast as he could. It wasn't too long before he ate himself right into the bag.

Up jumped Puss and pulled the bag shut tight! Then he marched off to the palace and asked to see the king.

"Your Majesty," he said, after bowing like a stylish courtier, "my lord, the Marquis of Carabas, has heard how fond you are of rabbit stew, so he has asked me to bring you this small token of his esteem!"

The king saw what was in the bag and was as pleased as punch. "By the way," he chuckled, "you might also mention to your master how fond I am of roast pheasant!"

It was no trouble at all for such a smart cat to catch a pheasant, and back he went to the palace. The king was more pleased than ever and said that he hoped some day to meet this thoughtful young nobleman who sent him such delicious gifts

"I am sure that can be arranged one day soon, Your Majesty," smiled Puss in Boots.

On his way out of the palace, he overheard the coachman complaining to the stable boy, "Here I was all ready to take this afternoon off, but now I'm told I must take the king and his daughter driving out to the lake!"

Puss ran all the way back to his young master. "Quick!" he cried. "Take off your

clothes and jump in the lake! Your fortune is about to be made even sooner than I expected!"

Puss hid the clothes under a rock and when he saw the royal carriage approaching, he ran to meet it, shouting, "Help! Help! Someone has robbed my lord, the Marquis of Carabas, while he was swimming in the lake!"

The king was shocked on hearing what had happened to his friend. He snapped his fingers and ordered his two footmen to fetch a rich suit of clothes from the palace and rush to the Marquis's rescue.

Now, Puss's master was quite a handsome young man, and once he was dressed in his fine new clothes, he looked every inch a dashing young nobleman.

The princess fell madly in love with him at first sight, and the king, noticing her reaction, offered to take the Marquis home in the royal carriage.

Meanwhile, Puss ran on ahead. Soon he came to a great stone castle —the home of the giant himself. Walking in boldly, he swept off his hat and bowed low to the wicked monster.

"Your Excellency," he said, "my lord, the Marquis of Carabas, ordered me not to pass by this way without paying his deepest respects to such a powerful magician as yourself!"

"Smart fellow," said the giant, who was seated at the table, eating.

"Still, I can hardly believe what he told me," Puss went on.

"And what might that be?"

"That you have the power to turn yourself into something as strong and fierce as a lion?"

"You think not? Watch!" With a roar, the giant turned himself into the king of beasts!

Puss in Boots pretended to tremble with fear. "Who c-c-could imagine such a th-thing!" he quavered. "Even so, I'll bet there's one thing that's beyond even *your* powers!"

"Try me," growled the giant.

"A lion is one thing," said Puss, "but there's no way anyone your size could turn himself into a tiny little mouse!"

"Guess again, fool!" And instantly the huge lion became a tiny, squeaking mouse.

In a flash, Puss in Boots pounced on him and gobbled him up—and that was the end of the Wicked Giant!

49

When the royal carriage rolled into the courtyard, Puss ran out to greet it. "Welcome to Carabas Castle, Your Majesty!" he announced. And to his young master, he added, "My lord, I have taken the liberty of having a great feast prepared in honor of your royal guests!"

"Well done, Puss!" grinned the handsome young nobleman.

The servants were so happy to be freed from the power of the Wicked Giant, they had indeed prepared the most delicious feast of their lives.

The feasting lasted long into the night,
[an]d before it was over, Puss in Boots took
[ca]re to show the king all the jewels and
[ot]her treasures stored in the castle.

By now, His Majesty felt sure he could
never find a worthier suitor for his
daughter's hand. So the very next day he
announced the engagement of the princess
to the Marquis of Carabas.

The wedding was celebrated with great pomp and ceremony. And guess what the happy peasants brought to their favorite feline? . . . a beautiful lady pussycat!

So Puss in Boots, too, was married along with his noble master, and they all lived happily ever after!

The Bremen Town Musicians

Once upon a time, there was a donkey that had grown too old to work. For many years it had carried heavy sacks of grain to the mill for its master. But now it was too feeble to tote such a load, so the miller and his wife began to talk about getting rid of the poor old thing.

The wife thought they should sell its hide. "At least that'll bring in a little money," she said, "to help us buy a younger animal."

But the miller was too kind-hearted for that. After all, the donkey had served him faithfully for a long time. So he took it out into the woods and fields where it could at least nibble a few thistles and blades of grass, and he left it there to shift for itself.

Now that it was all alone, the donkey
threw back its head and gave a loud
mournful bray. Its master had started back
to the mill, but the piercing sound brought
tears to his eyes. "Good-bye, old pal!" he
shouted back over his shoulder. "I'll never
find another donkey who can hee-haw like
that!"

His words made the donkey feel a good
deal better. As a matter of fact, it had
always secretly believed it could bray quite
beautifully. "Hmm, who knows—perhaps
I'm giving up hope too soon," the donkey
said to itself. "Why don't I become a
street musician? Maybe folks would pay
money to hear me sing!"

So first thing the next morning, the donkey set out for the nearby town of Bremen to seek its musical fortune. Before long it came to a dog that was stretched out alongside the road, panting for breath.

"What's wrong, old Bow-Wow?" said the donkey. "Aren't you one of the huntsman's hounds?"

"I was," said the dog, "but now I'm too old and weak to keep up with the pack, and the huntsman doesn't think I'm worth my keep. He was going to shoot me, so I ran as far and as fast as these old legs could carry me! But what am I to do now? I've nowhere to go and nothing to eat."

"Many's the time I've heard you barking and baying with the other hounds," said the donkey. "Can you still make that kind of music, like you did when the pack was on the scent?"

"Of course!" The dog lifted its head and gave a grand howl.

"Wonderful!" said the donkey. "Look here, I'm going to Bremen to become a town musician. Come with me, and we'll form a duet!"

"Sounds good to me," said the dog, and he trotted along with the donkey.

Pretty soon they came to a sad old pussycat that was crouched on a tree stump, drooping its head and meowing pitifully.

"How now, old Whiskers!" said the donkey. "What's your problem? Surely it can't be as bad as all that."

"I used to be the best mouser in these parts," said the pussycat, "but now my teeth have gotten dull, and I'm too old to chase mice. All I'm good for is purring by

the kitchen fire, so my mistress was going to drown me. I had to scamper for dear life, but what am I to do now? I've nowhere to go and nothing to eat."

"Remember how you used to yowl at night and serenade the cats at the mill?" said the donkey. "Why waste a talent like yours! Old Bow-Wow and I are on our way to Bremen to become street musicians. Come with us, and we'll form a trio."

"That's the best offer I've had yet," said the pussycat. "Count me in!"

A little way farther on, they came to a farm. An old rooster was perched on the gatepost, crowing his heart out.

"Aren't you a little mixed up?" asked the donkey. "It's not morning. Why all the cock-a-doodle-dooing this time of the afternoon?"

"The farmer thinks I'm too old and stringy to keep around the barnyard," sighed the rooster. "Tonight his wife's going to make chicken soup out of me, I thought I might as well crow while I s have the chance."

"Don't give up too soon," said the donkey. "Any fowl who can cock-a-doodl doo like you has a great future! We're o our way to become town musicians in Bremen. Come along with us, and we'll form a quartet!"

"Now you're talking," said the rooster. "That's more my style than a soup pot!"

The four friends traveled on. Darkness fell while they were going through the woods, so they stopped to rest for the night. The donkey and dog lay down at the foot of a tree, and the cat curled up on a tree limb. The rooster fluttered up to one of the higher branches. From here he could see a light in the distance.

"Looks like a house over that way," he called down. "Should we try to reach it?"

"Suits me," said the donkey. "Maybe there'll be a barn with some straw."

The cat and dog liked the idea, too.
The dog thought whoever lived there might spare him a bone, and the cat was hoping for a drop of milk. So they set out in the direction of the light.

Sure enough, it was coming from a house. The donkey peeked in the window.

"Who's in there?" asked the cat.

"A gang of robbers," said the donkey.

"They're having a feast. The table's loaded with all kinds of goodies!"

"O-o-oh!" the animals groaned hungrily, wishing they could have a bite or two for themselves.

The four friends put their heads together and came up with a plan to chase away the robbers. The donkey put his front hooves up on the window sill, and the dog and the cat jumped up on his back, and the rooster perched on the donkey's head.

When they were all ready, the donkey shouted, *"Sing!"* The donkey brayed, the dog barked and howled, the cat screeched, and the rooster crowed!

The robbers jumped up in terror and ran screaming out of the house.

The four friends sat down at the table and started gobbling everything in sight, agreeing it was the finest meal they'd ever tasted.

Then they put out the light and settled down to sleep.

Long after midnight, the robbers came out of their hiding place in the woods and sneaked closer to the house to see if it was safe to come back yet.

Everything seemed dark and quiet. The robber chief sent one of his gang to go see if the coast was clear.

The robber tiptoed up to the house and crept inside. He'd brought a candle along in his pocket and bent down to light it off a couple of live coals that had fallen onto the hearth. But those "live coals" were actually the cat's two eyes, glowing in the dark! Puss jumped at the robber with an angry yowl.

The man gave a yell of fear and darted for the door. As he dashed out of the house, the dog bit him on the leg, and as he ran across the yard, the donkey kicked him in the seat of the pants. Just then the rooster flew out of the house, crowing

"Cock-a-doodle-doo! Cock-a-doodle-doo!" at the top of its lungs.

By the time the robber got back to his pals, he was shivering and shaking with fright.

"What happened?" asked the chief.

"P-P-Plenty!" said the robber. "There's
a horrible old witch squatting on the
hearth. She snarled and tried to scratch my
eyes out with her long nails! Then a guard
by the door stabbed me in the leg, and a
hairy ogre in the yard almost brained me
with a club, but got me in the seat of my
pants instead! And just as I picked myself
up, the town judge came rushing out of
the house, shouting, "Catch the thief—do!
Take him to jail—do!"

That was enough for the rest of the gang. Without another word, they ran off through the woods!

That suited our four friends just fine. Now they had the house all to themselves—and for all we know, they could still be living there!

The Country Mouse

Once upon a time, in the country, there lived a tiny brown mouse. The country mouses's house was made out of an old hat, and it was cozy, warm and comfortable.

Outside of his house, the mouse hung a hammock between two branches of a tree, and he liked nothing better than to lie in the hammock and take long afternoon naps.

In the mornings, the country mouse would meet his friends and neighbors at a nearby brook, and together they would go into the woods to dig for nuts and acorns. They all worked very hard, but because they worked together, they always had fun and the mornings passed quickly.

First they would gather nuts and acorns and put them in big sacks. Then they would carry the sacks back home, and divide them up equally. There was always enough for everyone. Every once in a while, they would get tired of eating acorns and nuts, so the mouse and his friends would dig up some potatoes in their community potato patch. The country mouse liked nothing better than a hot roasted potato for dinner!

Every Saturday, the countryfolk would gather by the brook and have a picnic. After lunch, they'd swim in the brook, and go sailing on their homemade rafts. What fun they would have!

Life in the country was simple and peaceful and the country mouse was very happy.

One day, the country mouse received a letter from his mouse friend who lived in the city. The city mouse invited his friend to come for a visit!

The country mouse thought the big city must be an exciting place, and he missed his friend, so he decided to accept the invitation. He packed up a few belongings, said goodbye to his neighbors, and set off

70

The city was a very exciting place
indeed, filled with unusual sights. Soon, the
country mouse arrived at the city mouse's
home. The two friends were very happy to
see one another. "You must be hungry
and tired after your journey," said the city
mouse, and the two sat down to a very
fancy dinner.

"Now for dessert!" cried the city mouse, when they'd finished their meal. "Come with me!" and he led the country mouse into a pantry filled with goodies.

"I'll bet you can't find such treats in the country!" boasted the city mouse. And the country mouse had to agree that cupcakes and cheese were certainly more unusual than roasted potatoes!

Then the city mouse led his friend
through a hole at the bottom of the pantry
wall. "This is my bedroom," he said. The
country mouse looked around the cold,
bare room, and couldn't help thinking of
his own cozy bedroom back in the country.

"*Yowl!*"

"What was that?" asked the country
mouse.

"Just the house cat. Don't worry, he
can't get through the doorway," said the
city mouse. "*Scat!*" he told the peeking
cat.

The country mouse still felt a little
scared.

After a troubled night's sleep, the country mouse awoke still tired. "Stop!" cried the city mouse, as the country mouse started out the bedroom doorway. "Look," the city mouse told his friend. "The cook always puts mousetraps down early in the morning. We have to creep out very carefully and quietly."

The city mouse led the country mouse along the walls, out the kitchen window, and down a drainpipe. My goodness, thought the country mouse, what a lot of bother to go through each day!

The country mouse followed his friend
around the city, looking at all the sights.
Somehow, just walking through the busy
streets and avoiding the traffic tired the
country mouse more than a whole morning
digging in the potato patch.

"Gruff!"

"Run!" shrieked the city mouse. "It's
the neighbor's dog!" The two friends ran
fast and hard and finally hid inside the
drainpipe, where the dog couldn't find
them.

Shivering inside the cold drainpipe, the
country mouse decided it was time for him
to go home.

He thanked his friend for having him, and suggested that for the next visit, the city mouse should come to the country.

"It may not be as exciting as the city," the country mouse told his friend, "but it certainly is a lot more peaceful!"

That night the country mouse snuggled happily in his own bed, listening to the night sounds of the country. He was very glad to be home.

The Baby Duck

Once there was a mama duck and
Mama Duck's nest was well hidden among
the reeds that bordered the pond. The six
eggs in it were due to hatch very soon.
She knew the woods were full of hungry
creatures who would love to get at her
little darlings, so every now and then she
would take a walk around outside the reeds
to make sure no bad guys were coming.

The next time she was gone, one of the eggs cracked open—even sooner than expected—and out popped a baby duck! His name was Keeko, because that's what his mama had decided to call the first of her brood to hatch.

Keeko was surprised that no one was around to celebrate such an important event. But he didn't let that dishearten him. He stepped over the other eggs and wandered out of the nest to see what he could see.

Everything looked new and wonderful to Keeko—especially a pretty-colored bird up in a tree, who filled the forest with happy songs.

"Who are you?" asked Keeko, "and how is it you can sing so well?"

"I'm a bird, can't you see? And that's why I can sing so well."

"What about me? Do you know who I am and if I can sing?"

"You're just a silly little duck," said the bird and flew off with a flap of its wings.

Keeko was a bit crestfallen over the
unfriendly way the bird had answered him.
But he soon noticed a cricket making
music in the grass.

"Are you a bird, too?" asked the
duckling.

The insect looked somewhat put out.
"For your information," it snapped, "I'm a
cricket—and I only sing when others leave
me in peace!"

More dejected than ever, Keeko walked on until he met a rabbit who was digging a tunnel. This time, when he opened his bill, he tried to sound a little older and smarter, as if he knew all about the creatures of the woods.

But the rabbit didn't even listen. "Look," he interrupted, "if you want to make yourself useful, put a tray of this loose dirt on your head and carry it as far away as possible!"

The poor duckling didn't realize the rabbit just wanted to get rid of him, so he did as he was told and kept on walking all night! At daybreak he finally stopped when he saw a little dormouse gathering nuts, berries and acorns among the roots of an oak tree.

Keeko tried to tell him what had happened, but as soon as he opened his mouth, the dormouse fell asleep. Keeko felt terribly downcast. It seemed as if no one would ever pay any attention to him.

He walked and walked until he came to a meadow, where a timid fawn was nibbling clover.

"Hello," he said. "I'm a little duck. I've met a bird who can sing very well. Crickets can sing, too, but I don't like them. A rabbit didn't want to sing, and a dormouse just fell asleep. Would you sing with me?"

"I don't know how to sing," said the fawn. And then, for fear their voices might attract other animals or hunters, it gave a quick jump and disappeared into the woods.

Keeko was getting desperate. Wouldn't
he ever meet anyone friendly? To make
matters worse, as he walked on, his tummy
began to feel uncomfortably empty.

Just then he came to some sunflowers.
They looked like huge plates of seeds. The
tallest one bent down and whispered:

"We know you're hungry, and we're
very thirsty! We'll wither away if someone
doesn't water our roots soon. If you would
please bring us water, we'll feed you!"

Keeko jumped with joy and began bringing water from a nearby pond in a nutshell.

The lovely sunflowers soaked it up greedily. Bit by bit, they began to straighten their stalks and stand taller. To the poor little duckling, it seemed as if those plates of seeds were growing farther and farther away from him. Was he just being made fun of again?

But the sunflowers smiled happily and began raining down a shower of yummy black seeds!

Keeko pecked them all up, and as soon
as his tummy was full, he began to quack
out a funny little song.

It didn't have much of a tune, but it
was loud enough to be heard by Big Bad
Fox, who could hardly believe he was
being invited to sample such a tasty
mouthful!

The tall sunflowers could see danger
coming. "Shh! Stop singing, little duck!"
they warned. "Run away fast or the fox
will gobble you up in one bite!"

Keeko was frightened half to death and ran as fast as his little legs could carry him! The poor baby duck could feel the fox's hot breath almost singeing his downy little feathers. He reached the pond and jumped in—just in the nick of time!

Imagine his joy when he saw a cluster
of little baby ducklings just like himself on
the other side of the pond!

They were his little brothers, who had
hatched after Keeko left the nest.

Our hero swam toward them eagerly!

At last he could celebrate his birthday properly—with a loud chorus of quack, quacks—under the watchful and loving eye of Mama Duck!

The Selfish Rabbit

Once there was a bunny rabbit named Toby who loved vegetables. He knew every farmer's garden for miles around, so whenever he wanted an ear of corn or a nice bunch of juicy carrots, he would go and help himself. Scarecrows didn't frighten him a bit.

Being a greedy little rabbit, Toby would never share his food with any of the other wildfolk, no matter how hungry they might be.

One day he was enjoying a delicious
lunch of corn on the cob. He didn't know
a bird named Flitter was peeking at him
from behind some leaves.

The corn looked so good that poor little
Flitter's beak was watering. He knew there
was no use asking Toby for a bite—so
suddenly he darted forward and snapped up
a couple of corn kernels!

Toby was furious. "Stop thief!" he yelled and chased after Flitter.

That bunny rabbit could run like the wind! But he had no chance of catching Flitter, who just flew up to the top of a big oak tree. So did Flitter's friends after they, too, snatched a few corn kernels in their beaks.

Toby was smart enough to figure out
that if he ever hoped to catch a bird, he
would need wings. That gave him an idea.

The day before, at a fair in a nearby
town, a boy had lost his balloon. It had
floated away until its string caught in some
bushes. Toby ran to look for it.

Sure enough, there was the red balloon,
still in the bushes!

Toby pulled the string loose and tied it to a stick. Then he held on tight and gave a big jump. Up, up soared the balloon!

Now if he could just steer it toward the top of that oak tree where Flitter and his friends were perching . . . .

But those smart little birds didn't wait
for the balloon to come to *them*. They
swooped down and pecked it with their
beaks until—*pop!*—the balloon burst.

"Oh, oh!" thought Toby. He gulped
with fear as he felt himself falling . . .
faster and faster!

Ker-splash! He landed right in the
middle of a duck pond!

To make matters worse, the water felt icy cold.

Luckily for Toby, some ducklings were paddling around in the pond. Somehow they managed to pull him out and lay him gently on a big lily pad. Then they pushed it ashore.

Shivering and shaking, poor Toby
dragged himself home and crawled under
the covers.

There he lay, coughing and sneezing,
with his eyes watering, reliving every
moment of his unhappy balloon flight. He
thought gloomily how Flitter and his friends
and all the other woodland creatures must
be laughing at him!

Dr. Hedgehog said Toby had a high fever. "But don't worry—I brought along just the right medicine, made of pepper and red ants and castor oil. It works wonders in cases like yours!"

"Get away from me!" groaned Toby. "I'm not going to take any uggy stuff like that!"

So Dr. Hedgehog went away, sulking.

Toby lay in bed moaning out loud, "If only the Wise Old Elf were here. *He'd* know what to do."

Guess who heard him? Flitter and his friends! They were worried about poor Toby and wanted to make up for the trouble they had caused him.

So they flew swiftly to the Wise Old Elf's mushroom house and begged him to whip up one of his miracle mixtures to cure the sick bunny.

The Wise Old Elf set to work at once in his laboratory. He looked up a recipe in his Book of Magic and chanted a spell for sick bunnies while he stirred the mixture. Then he hurried to Toby's bedside.

"Swallow this!" he ordered.

Toby did and it tasted delicious. After one spoonful, he felt so much better, he somersaulted right out of bed!

"Aha!" cried the Wise Old Elf. "A miracle cure like this calls for a celebration!"

So he made a big bowlful of the yummiest pudding you ever tasted, and all the forest folk were invited to the party!

Toby had a special reason to celebrate. He knew now that Flitter and the others hadn't been laughing at him—they had gone out of their way to help him!

"How dumb I was, making such a fuss over those measly little corn kernels!" he thought. "The most wonderful thing in the world are kind-hearted friends who help each other out!"

The Little Clown

Once there was a Little Clown who wanted, more than anything else in the world, to cheer people up and make them laugh. But whenever he tried to do his circus tricks, no one would stop and watch him or even seemed to care.

So one day the Little Clown packed his bag and set out to seek his fortune.

"Maybe someday I can be in a real circus," he said to himself wistfully.

He walked and walked till he came to a
big forest. Before he could find his way
through the woods, it got dark. The Little
Clown was all tired out. Wrapping himself
in a blanket, he stretched out under a tree
and fell fast asleep, with his toy stuffed
dog, Tweety Pup, standing guard at his
feet.

When the Little Clown woke up the next morning, he washed in a nearby brook. Birds in the trees twittered with amazement. His clown face seemed to wash right off! Underneath the paint was a . . . *boy!*

The news spread like wildfire, and other woodland creatures came to see this strange person with two faces.

How excited and astonished they were when the Little Clown did his morning exercises. He grabbed a tree branch and swung around it as if he were performing on a circus trapeze!

A little bear began to imitate him when he walked on his hands with his legs in the air.

It was the Little Clown's turn to be amazed when the bear did the same trick on just one paw!

The Little Clown was so happy to find
an audience who liked his circus tricks that
he began to play a lively march on his
horn.

Two squirrels danced in time to the
music. Then other animals joined in, and
soon all the wildfolk were frolicking about
the Little Clown and having fun.

Afterward, a squirrel jumped up on the Little Clown's knee and asked, "How does it happen you can do such wonderful things?"

"Because I'm a circus clown!" the funny little boy replied.

But the most wonderful thing of all, he thought, was how much the woodland folk had enjoyed his performance. He had finally made someone laugh and have fun!

Of course the animals had never heard
of circuses, so he told them all about the
Big Top and the acrobats and dancers and
clowns and jugglers who traveled around so
people could watch them perform.

The animals were so interested they
decided to form a circus of their own!

They practiced and practiced until they felt sure they were ready. Then the Little Clown blew his horn and led them into town. It was just like a real circus parade—except that the star performers were animals!

Children came running to watch. They were so excited and eager to see the show that they got their parents to put up a tent and make costumes and everything else that was needed.

At last the show was about to begin!
One after another, the animal circus stars
went through their stunts.

At a word from the Little Clown, his
trained beavers dove through the hoop.
Bears balanced on one paw. Daredevil
squirrels swung by their tails from the
flying trapeze and somersaulted high in the
air!

But the real show-stopper was a magic act in which an animal magician pulled yards and yards of ribbon out of the pelican's beak—and then little birds flew out, singing and swooping over the heads of the audience!

Children laughed and clapped and
whistled. The whole tent shook with
applause! Everyone loved the Little Clown's
jokes and tricks, and thought his animal
circus was the greatest show they had ever
seen.

He led his woodland stars from town to
town, performing wherever they went. With
the money they earned, they were able to
buy enough food to last them all through
the winter until the spring flowers returned.

Then the Little Clown's animal friends
returned to the forest and he went in
search of another circus to join.

All this happened long ago. But the day finally came when the Little Clown became famous and joined a big circus that traveled all over the world. And wherever he went, guess who stood guard outside his tent?

Yep, that's right—his toy stuffed dog, Tweety Pup!

The Squirrel with Green Spots

Skippy was a little squirrel who lived with his mama and three brothers in a hollow tree. Every morning, Mama Squirrel would tell her children to go out and gather nuts for the winter, but Skippy never minded her.

As soon as he left the house, he would
go running and jumping and dancing
through the dewy grass and sweet-smelling
flowers.

Often, he would scamper down to the
pond to make music with the frogs,
because Skippy loved music.

He also loved all kinds of sweets.

121

One of his favorite kinds were cherries. He would get his pal, Twit-Twit the sparrow, to fly up into the branches of a cherry tree and peck loose the stems of the ripest, juiciest cherries he could see.

As fast as they fell to the ground, Skippy would gobble them up . . . until he had a bulging little tummyful!

By the time he got home at sundown, Skippy would be all dirty and sticky with cherry juice.

Mama Squirrel would just sigh and shake her head and roll up her sleeves. And then she'd dunk the little chap in a tub full of water and soapsuds. Oh, what weeping and wailing would echo through the woodland—because Skippy *hated* water!

The next day was a beautiful autumn day and Mabel the Turtle told her friends some sensational news.

"You know that deep dark cave on the other side of the pond? Well, Ricky Rabbit says that's the den of a terrible bear—and he's got a store of delicious honey hidden inside his cave!"

"*Honey!* Ooh wow, my favorite treat!" exclaimed Skippy. "That's where I'm heading right now, pals! Who wants to come along?"

Mabel, being the slowest, decided to swim across the pond to the cave. Twit-Twit said he'd fly there. But Skippy hated water so much, he had to go clear around the pond to get to the other side.

That didn't mean it would take him long to get there, though. No, indeed—he went swinging through the trees like Tarzan!

Skippy had such fun zooming from branch to branch, he forgot where he was going. He ended up lost in the middle of the forest and had to ask a polite old owl the way back to the pond.

Well, to make a long story short, Skippy reached the cave zippety-quick. And he didn't waste a minute worrying about that terrible bear whose den it was—he just walked right in!

Sure enough, inside the cave was a huge jar of honey! The only way Skippy could get at it was to jump up on a stool and stick his head down in the jar.

You can imagine how that greedy little squirrel went to work, slurping up the sweet stuff. He slurped so fast, his tongue got tired, and he had to stop and lift his head to give it a rest.

Just then he heard heavy steps outside. Oh, oh! thought Skippy. That can't be Twit-Twit, or Mabel either! They don't sound like that when they move around!

127

The greedy little squirrel was shaking with fright. "It must be the bear!" he gulped. "What'll I do now?"

Looking around, Skippy saw a bag of supplies. He jumped into it just in time— because the very next moment, in walked the bear! Not a big terrible bear, just a small fat boy bear.

Boy Bear knew right away someone had been at his honey—and what about that bag of precious green beans he'd been storing up for the winter?

He rushed over to look into the bag—
and gave a yelp of fright. Because up
popped the strangest animal he'd ever seen,
covered all over with green spots!

Boy Bear was scared out of his wits,
and so was Skippy! They both burst out of
the cave and ran in opposite directions!

Skippy, you see, had got himself so
smeared with honey that the green beans
in the bag were sticking all over him. But
Boy Bear was too terrified to stop and take
a closer look—and so was Skippy!

129

Skippy didn't stop running till he reached a thick clump of bushes. When he finally got up enough courage to peek out, guess what he saw? There were his brothers, gathering nuts like good little squirrels.

Skippy heaved a sigh of relief and called, "Hi, fellas!" But his brothers took one look at that weird creature in the bushes and ran home screeching!

"Oh, golly!" thought Skippy as he looked down at his green spots. "I wonder what Mama will do when she sees me?"

One thing she didn't do was get scared.
She knew right away this was her naughty
little son. She gave him a hug and a kiss
and a spank, and then she took him home
and scrubbed him good and proper till all
the honey and green beans came off.

Ever since then, Skippy has been a model little squirrel. Every morning, he washes his face and combs his hair, and then goes out with Twit-Twit and Mabel to gather nuts.

Oh, yes, he's still very fond of honey—but only when his mama serves it at home.

Suzy the Doll

There once was a pretty little doll
named Suzy who lived in a big city full of
people and cars. At night when Marinella,
the girl who owned her, was asleep, Suzy
loved to look through travel books. Her
favorite ones had pictures of meadows and
woods and brooks and farms.

How lovely it would be to live there,
she thought, with butterflies and birds all
around.

One spring day, Marinella's parents
decided to go for a drive in the country.
Suzy gazed, wide-eyed, out the window at
all the wonderful sights—at the trees and
farms and green pastures where cows and
sheep grazed peacefully.

All of a sudden, the car went over a
bump. Suzy was jolted out the open
window and landed at the edge of a field!

Hurray!, she thought. Just the kind of place I always wanted to be!

Jumping to her feet, Suzy scampered toward the woods. There she met two little animals who were sobbing unhappily.

"Who are you? And why are you crying?" asked Suzy.

"I'm Tim the Dormouse," said the smallest one, "and he's Sammy Squirrel. We're crying because Spud the Farm Dog won't let us play in the barnyard any more."

"Why not?" asked Suzy.

"Because he's so lazy! Every night while he's asleep, little chicks and ducklings disappear. Spud doesn't know who's taking them, so he blames us—and we're his only friends!"

Suzy felt sure they were telling the truth and wanted to help them. So she walked along a path at the edge of a brook that led to the farm. In the barnyard she met Spud, a plump, funny little watchdog.

Suzy and Spud became friends right away. They talked and talked about the strange disappearance of the chicks and ducklings. Neither one could imagine what had happened to them.

By the time it got dark, Suzy was feeling drowsy from her day in the open air. Spud politely let her lie down in his roomy doghouse while he stood guard outside. Before long, they were both sound asleep.

The next morning, Spud trotted around
the farmyard making his usual check to see
if everything was all right. A duckling and
a chick were crying their eyes out. "Oh,
oh!" gulped the little watchdog. "Something
tells me this means bad news!"

When he asked them what was the
matter, the duckling sobbed, "Last night,
all our brothers and sisters disappeared!
We're the only ones left!"

And the chick added, "Wait'll the
farmer finds out—you'll be in big trouble!"

When Suzy heard the news, she knew she had to do something fast to discover the real robber. She had a hunch that if anyone might be able to come up with a clue, it was the gossipy little birds of the forest. They saw and heard everything!

She was right. The birdies were eager to help. After much soft twittering and chirping, they and Suzy worked out a secret plan to trap the robber.

Toward sundown, the birds perched in trees along a path that the Big Bad Fox took every evening. They knew he was the worst crook in the forest. As soon as they saw him coming with his bag slung over his shoulder, they began to chatter loudly to one another:

"Have you heard the news? The farmer got a whole new flock of tender little chicks and ducklings today!"

The Fox heard everything, but he didn't say a word—he just chuckled to himself.

141

He waited till night had fallen. Then, when the moon was high in the sky and all the lights at the farm were out, he sneaked through the fence and headed toward the barnyard. Spud was snoring away as usual, sound asleep.

Without making the slightest sound, the Fox opened the door of the chicken coop and slipped inside. His mouth was already watering.

"Yum, yum!" he said to himself. "What a delicious dinner I'm going to have tonight!"

But what a surprise—the cage was empty! And just then, Suzy and Tim and Sammy jumped out of their hiding places and locked the door of the chicken coop!

Imagine the look on Big Bad Fox's face when he realized he was trapped! And he knew what would happen when the farmer found him there in the morning.

"Oh please, please! Let me out!" the Fox begged. "If you let me go, I promise I'll never come back to the farm ever again!"

143

"Well now, we *might* consider letting you out," said Suzy, "if you'll tell us what you did with all the chicks and ducklings you've been stealing."

"I will, I will!" the Fox whined. And he told her exactly where to find his secret den. He had been keeping the tasty little creatures there in preparation for a big feast.

At daybreak, Suzy woke up Spud and sent him out in the woods. He soon came back proudly with all the missing little chicks and ducklings.

The farmer was so pleased, he gave
Spud an extra big bowlful of dogfood that
day!

Ever since, Suzy has lived happily on
the farm. She tends the garden and, oh,
how she loves the fresh air and sunshine
and green grass and trees and all the farm
animals!

Spud snoozes as much as ever, but the farm folk don't worry about the Big Bad Fox any more.

Do you know why? Because Suzy the Doll is smarter than any old Fox!

The King of the Forest

One morning, Buster Bear woke up early. Instead of waiting for his mama to take him for their usual walk in the woods, Buster decided to go out by himself.

Mr. Hedgehog saw the little bear and scolded him. "Go home! You're not old enough to be out in the woods all alone!"

"Oh yes I am!" retorted Buster, who didn't like being talked to as if he was just a little toddler. "I'm big and strong! I'm the king of the forest!"

Just then a chestnut hit him right on the nose! Buster let out a yelp because it scared the wits out of him—and hurt a little bit, too.

The joker who threw it was a mischievous squirrel. "Want some breakfast?" he asked, jumping down from a branch.

"Sure," said Buster.

"Okay, I'm smart and you're strong. Together we can get lots of food. I'll show you how. Start shaking that tree over there!"

Buster shook it so hard, a lot of nuts fell down. But the squirrel gobbled all of them up.

"Wait a second," said Buster. "You're stuffing yourself, but what am I going to eat?"

"See the two bumblebees sipping from those flowers?" said the sly little squirrel. "Follow them, and I guarantee you'll find some delicious breakfast!"

So Buster did and, sure enough, the bees led him straight to a nice juicy honeycomb in a hollow oak tree.

"Yum, yum!" drooled Buster Bear. He stuck both paws in and started gorging on the delicious honey.

Next thing he knew, a whole swarm of bees came buzzing at him angrily, stinging him on his nose, which was all smeared with honey.

"Ow! Yow! Ouch!" yelled Buster and ran away as fast as he could.

"What you need is some nice cool water," said the squirrel, trying not to laugh at Buster.

He took the little bear down to the river, and he was right—when Buster stuck his head in, his poor swollen nose felt much better. But he also got quite a scare, because just then a strange animal popped up out of the water.

"Don't be scared," it said. "Haven't you ever seen a beaver before? Let's all be friends!"

153

Buster was always glad to find a new friend.

"From the look of your nose," said the beaver, "honey's not good for little bears. You should try eating fish. I've always heard that bears *love* fish!"

"Okay, but where can I find some?" Buster asked.

"No problem. Follow me!" He led Buster and the squirrel to his boat . . . but it looked awfully old and leaky.

The beaver proudly invited them aboard.

"No, thanks," said the squirrel. "I don't think I care to go fishing in a leaky old tub like that—especially since I can't swim!"

"Aw, you're just a little scaredy-cat," said Buster. He climbed in and the beaver paddled off. "Boats don't scare me, 'cause I'm a brave, strong bear. I'm the king of the forest!"

The current carried the boat along faster and faster. Buster kept remembering what the squirrel had said.

"Uh, by the way," he asked his new friend, "can you tell me what *swimming* is?"

"Sure, I'll show you," said the beaver, diving into the water. "Just jump in headfirst and move your legs around—like this!"

Poor Buster never got a chance to try, because the boat was heading straight for a sunken tree! *Biffety-bang-boom!* It crashed into the trunk and broke all apart!

Buster barely managed to grab a branch and hang on for dear life to keep from getting dunked.

He looked so funny that the fish even jumped out of the water to laugh at him!

All the same, Buster was in big trouble. Now it was the squirrel's and the beaver's turn to be scared out of their wits. If anything happened to that poor little bear, they knew what Mama Bear would do to them! So they dashed through the woods to get help.

When they found Buster's mama and
told her what had happened, she didn't
waste any breath scolding them. She
jumped up and ran to the river like a
furry streak of lightning!

When she reached the riverbank, she
plunged in and swam out to the tree trunk
with a couple of swift strokes, grabbed
Buster by the scruff of the neck, and
brought him safely ashore!

Then she kissed him and gave him two spanks and sent him home, while his animal friends all giggled—but not loud enough for Mama Bear to hear them.

All that was a long time ago. Buster's animal friends don't giggle at him any more. They don't dare to, because he's too big and strong. In fact, whenever they're in trouble, *he*'s the one they go to for help.

Nowadays, you see, Buster Bear really *is* the king of the forest!

The Spoiled Puppy

There once was a spoiled puppy named Bruce. Just because he came from a long line of pedigreed dogs, he put on airs and acted as if he were better than other animals.

The sad truth was that, ever since he was born, his parents and owners had cuddled him and made a fuss over him— so Bruce thought he could do whatever he pleased.

Before long, he took to staying out all night and palling around with a couple of bad dogs named Spike and Mugsy. In fact, Bruce wanted to be their leader! Since he never got scolded or spanked, he paid no attention to anything his parents told him.

Spike and Mugsy had often been in trouble with farmers for raiding chicken coops and tearing up gardens. So Bruce began picking up all their bad habits, too.

Children were scared of them, and cats didn't dare stick their noses outdoors when those three were around!

One night, on the way back from their usual mischief-making, they came to a big ditch. Spike and Mugsy jumped over it and kept on going, but Bruce landed, *ker-splash*, right in the muddy water!

What a time he had crawling out of that ditch! When he finally climbed up on the other side, he was dirty enough to scare a wolf. Worse yet, the mud wouldn't rub off. As it dried, his hairs stuck out with slimy water weeds clinging to them.

A wise old owl hooted, "That's what happens to disobedient little animals—they always end up in a mess!"

When Bruce got home, his mama didn't even recognize him. She took one look and let out a howl of fear. "Help! There's a monster loose!"

Neighbors came running from all around. "I'm no monster!" the puppy kept yelling. "It's *me*—Bruce!"

But no one paid any attention or even heard him. People were too busy whacking him with brooms and sticks and canes.

Poor Bruce finally managed to escape by darting between their legs. He ran till his tongue was hanging out almost down to the ground. By now, he looked worse than ever with all his bruises and swellings.

As he hobbled along, whom should he see but his two pals. "Spike! Mugsy!" he called, hoping for a little sympathy.

They didn't recognize him, either. They ran like frightened pussycats—terrified of this strange-looking beast who knew their names.

"No one likes me any more," Bruce whined. "Where can I go?"

Stumbling along in the darkness, he lost his footing and fell into a millstream.

"Oh, no!" the puppy moaned. "Not twice in one night!"

But this dunking turned out to be a lucky break! The more he splashed and floundered around in the water, the more mud and gooey weeds washed off him. By the time he reached shore, he was all nice and clean again!

"Better run home, Bruce!" the little birds and wildfolk warned. "There's a terrible monster prowling around these woods!"

"No problem," the puppy replied. "I'll scare that thing off, and he won't *ever* come back.

Bruce's mama hadn't slept a wink. When he finally got home, she ran and hugged him, in spite of all his sore spots and scrapes and bruises. "Oh, my dear little Brucie boy!" she sobbed. "I was afraid that awful monster had gotten you!"

"Don't worry, Mama dear," he replied. "It was a hard fight, but I chased him away, and he'll never bother us again!"

She was so proud of her brave boy, she made him a yummy feast!

171

Bruce's mama even gave a party in her son's honor. All his friends brought him presents and praised his courage.

There was someone up in a tree, however, who knew the truth, the whole truth, and nothing but the truth—and that was the wise old owl.

"One should never tell a lie, Bruce," he
hooted, "but if you'll promise to be a
good, obedient little dog from now on, I'll
never tell anyone what *really* happened!"

Bruce promised, and from that day on,
he began a new life.

Now he always obeys his mama, and whenever his master takes him out for a walk, Bruce trots along at his side like a well-trained doggy should. And guess what else?

He doesn't hang around with Spike and Mugsy anymore, either!

Gary Groundhog's Narrow Escape

Once upon a time there lived a mama groundhog with three children. One day, Mama Groundhog decided her three children were old enough to make homes of their own.

"Remember to dig your burrows deep," she told them, "and be sure to have a front door and back door, so you can escape in case of danger!"

Gary Groundhog just yawned. He was her youngest child and often didn't listen to what his mama told him.

"Why bother with two doors?" Gary
shrugged. "After all, I'm just a little
groundhog. One door is enough for me."

"Don't be foolish!" a friendly bird
scolded him. "Two doors are very
important. That way, if someone bad comes
in one door, you can get out the other
way, all safe and sound!"

But Gary still wouldn't listen.

177

First he dug his burrow with his sharp little claws. One of his squirrel friends helped by shoveling away the loose soil Gary dug out. Then a rabbit helped him saw the wood he needed to make his furniture.

When it was all finished, Gary was proud of his new home. By now he was pretty tired, so he stretched out in the sun to rest a bit.

Just then, Sleepy, the wise old
dormouse, passed by. "Snug little home
you've got there, my boy," he remarked.
"It'll be a nice safe hideaway when you
put in two doors."

"There'll only be one door," said Gary.
"Wait'll you see how beautiful it will
look!"

179

The next day, Gary made the door to his burrow. He painted it red with strawberry juice.

"Hmm . . . very pretty," he said to himself, "but I want it to look even prettier!"

So he planted some golden yellow daisies on one side of the door, and purple thistles on the other.

"How do you like my door?" he asked Little Bear.

"It's beautiful. But I've always heard that groundhog burrows have *two* doors."

"Not this one!" snapped Gary. "I'm young and quick on my feet. Whenever there's danger, I'll always have plenty of time to get away!"

Little Bear didn't argue. But he didn't look very convinced, either. He just shook his head and walked away.

"Phooey on him!" thought Gary to himself. "He's not a groundhog. What does he know?"

And then, just to show he didn't care what other people thought, Gary stretched out in a hammock and prepared to enjoy a little snooze in the sunshine.

All of a sudden Gary heard furious
barking. He sat bolt upright. "Oh, oh," he
gulped. "What's that?"

It didn't take long to find out. Jumping
out of his hammock, Gary stood up tall on
his hind legs, the way groundhogs do, to
see what was going on.

A big, fierce-looking dog was running
straight toward him! Gary ducked into his
burrow fast and slammed the door!

183

But that wouldn't stop the dog for long. Gary could hear the awful creature hurling itself against his beautiful door! THUMP! . . . THUD! . . . CRASH!

The poor little groundhog was trembling with fear. How wrong he had been not to follow his mama's advice! Now he knew for sure why *two* doorways were so important!

Just when everything seemed hopeless, a wall of his tunnel broke apart—and there was old Mr. Hedgehog! Sensing Gary's danger, he had swiftly dug an escape tunnel to save his little friend!

"This way!" said Mr. Hedgehog, and
Gary didn't need any urging. He scurried
to safety through his friend's tunnel.

When they were out in the open air
again, Gary could see a hunter and his
dog walking away in the distance. Only
then did he dare go back and look at his
burrow. His lovely red door was ruined,
and his golden daisies and purple thistles
were all trampled. Even some of his
furniture had been smashed.

A little bird flew through the woods, telling the other animals what had happened. They all hurried to Gary's burrow.

"You should have paid attention to your mama," said a squirrel.

And the dormouse nodded, "Yes, indeed, my boy—you should always listen to those who are older and wiser than you."

"I know, I know! I'm sorry!" sobbed the little groundhog.

"Don't cry, Gary," said a little rabbit, patting Gary's shoulder. "If you like, I'll help you fix up your burrow."

"We'll all help you!" cried the other wildfolk.

And the next day, when Mama Groundhog came to visit her son, she saw that Gary had made *two* doors to his burrow—a beautiful front door for going in, and another, very simple door for leaving in a hurry.

"That's my good little boy!" she said, hugging him.

And Gary danced around happily, singing:

187

"It's a mighty snug burrow
Without any doubt!
I've a way to go in
And a way to get out!"

The End